Fundamentals of the Golf Swing:

Basic Building Blocks to the Complete Fundamental Golf Swing

Forward

They say that if you are not learning, you are not really living, and this couldn't be truer than when it comes to golf. Because whether you are a PGA tour pro or a complete novice, there is always something new you can learn to better your game. And of all the things you can learn and refine, that ever coveted, perfect golf swing, is no doubt a top priority on your list.

No matter where you may be on your golf journey this book serves to highlight some basic fundamentals that will help you improve your golf swing. When these fundamentals are utilized you can greatly improve the reliability of your shots and achieve a low scoring game on the green; wouldn't that be great? You will no longer have to be embarrassed on the golf course.

Think of this book as the kind and patient personal trainer that you have been looking for. In the exquisite details of the exercises and tutorials presented in this book you can learn what you have been missing out on without any shame. You will master a lot more than your swing, with this book as your guide you will master your confidence and find a whole new way to approach the game of golf.

This book will teach you how to:

- Improve your Grip
- Learn to control your Tempo
- Develop your Swing Sequence
- Correct Your Posture
- And much more!

Table of Contents

Introduction: Why You Bought this Book...4

Chapter 1: Get a Grip..5

    Strong Grip 6

    Neutral Grip 6

    Weak Grip 6

Chapter 2: Mastering the Sequence of the Swing..7

    Use Your Swing Trigger...7

    Go to Your Takeaway 8

    Orient Clubhead to the Right Plane 8

    Open your Club Head 8

    Keep Your Club in Check in the Middle of Your Backswing.................................8

    Look to Your Right..8

    Turn Your Lower Body 9

    Release and Straighten Your Right Arm 9

    Tense the Muscles on Your Left Side...9

    Make Full Rotation of Your Body as Your Club Impacts the Golf Ball 9

    End With Hand Raised Above Shoulder 9

Chapter 3: Working On Your Posture 10

    The Pre-Address Position 10

    Address Position 10

    Have Enough Axis Tilt at Address 10

Chapter 4: The Impact of Your Type of Golf Club on Your Swing 11

    Woods 11

    Irons 11

    Hybrids 11

    Wedges 11

Chapter 5: Understanding the Concept of a Swing Plane 12

    Two Planes of Golfing Existence! 12

    Mastering the One-Plane Method 12

    Mastering the Two-Plane Method 13

    Which Swing Plane is Best? 13

Chapter 6: Keeping Up the Proper Pace, Rhythm, and Tempo 13

    The Tempo Test 13

    Build Rhythm 14

Chapter 7: Making the Best of Your Stance, Alignment and Footwork. 14

    Stance 14

    Alignment 14

    Footwork 15

Conclusion: It's Elementary my Dear Watson 15

Introduction: Why You Bought this Book

Please don't take this the wrong way, but I think I can safely assume from the fact that you bought this book, that you have had some rough days out at the course in the not to distant past. Am I right? Well in that case you have bought the right book! Most books on this subject either sugar coat the harsh realities of golf or they streamline and steamroll through the more complex nuances of the subject so fast that you are left breathless in your incomprehension! Pretty tragic set of circumstances isn't it?

But it doesn't have to be that way! And this book seeks to avoid both of these ill advised fates. This book gets straight to the point and it delivers you the goods. In these chapters you will get the full course of meat and potatoes when it comes to knowing how to stand, how to move your arms and feed, and what clubs to use. These are simple but crucially important aspects of golf that every enthusiast needs to understand. You don't have to be bogged down by too many technical details, because in this book all you really need to know are the fundamentals of the swing!

Chapter 1: Get a Grip

Next, to your actual swing, having the right kind of grip your golf club is probably the most important part of the game. In doing this, you have to understand the difference between a strong, neutral, and a weak grip. And if you don't believe me, just take it from golfing phenom Ben Hogan. He realized the difference a good grip could make all the way back in the 1950's!

Even though Hogan retired in 1974, and passed away in 1997, he will be long remembered for his superb grip of the golf club for a long time afterwards. Tiger Woods has even cited Hogan as being the only player who could truly control the ball. Hogan gained this control by understanding that a slightly weak grip would enable him to control his swing in a specific way while he managed to hit the ball as hard as possible.

He learned how to manipulate his grip, shifting between weak, neutral, and strong, all in order to maximize his potential in any situation that the golf course threw at him. If there were water hazard he would loosen his grip for maneuverability, and if there was a sand trap he just might strengthen it to power right through!

I realize of course, that some of you may not know how to tell the difference between grips. So let's start off with one—quite literal—rule of thumb to help us out. Because the determination of what kind of grip you use will be based almost completely upon the placement of your index finger and your thumb in the traditional "V" grip formation. Now let's take a closer look at these variations and their effects upon our golf swing.

Strong Grip

In a grip that is strong, this V formation is placed right at the center of the shaft of your club. In this position the knuckles on your left hand (if you're a right handed golfer) should be visible to you as you look down at the ball. This strong grip has quite a few different inherent benefits in its use. For one thing it helps those who use it to more easily draw the ball and prevents the user from "slicing the ball". Perhaps you have heard this dreaded phrase tossed around on the golf course?

Well, if you wondered what all those golf veterans were talking about, allow me to demystify you. This is "golf-speak" for the action of glancing your golf club's face off-center causing you to adversely curve the shot. The strong grip prevents this from happening by allowing the face of the club to properly close prior to a shot, creating a more natural kind of draw. But you have to do it right, because if you are too forceful you could ruin your whole swing and turn it into disastrous hook that goes nowhere!

__Neutral Grip__

This kind of grip is used by those who generally have a better grasp (pun completely intended) of their golf game than others. The neutral grip places the knuckles of your hand in perfect alignment with the face of your golf club. You know your hands are placed in a neutral grip when you can see two of your left hand's knuckles in concert with the ball. Players that are able to use a neutral grip are better able to shape the direction that their ball will travel.

The great benefit of this is that you can largely eliminate the incidence of slicing your golf ball. This grip has been used well by many renowned golfers such as Jack Nicklaus and Tiger Woods, but for the rest of us mere mortals the neutral grip could come off as a bit unwieldy. It's not for everyone, but if you can get the hang of it, the neutral grip could really work some wonders for you.

Weak Grip

At first glance, you may be tempted to think that a weak grip is a bad thing. You probably lived your life thinking that a strong grip and a firm handshake were the best way to go right? But in golf this is not always the case. The weak grip manages to create a completely organic motion known as a "fade". This was the kind of grip that Hogan had mastered all those years ago in order to produce specific results when he wanted them.

This kind of grip seems to work especially well for those that have slow hips so that they can center their club face right as it strikes the golf ball. The weak grip is evident by only one of your knuckles being visible in concert with the ball. A weak grip helps keep you from falling into hook shots, and can give your ball much more backspin, allowing you to hit it much higher which is greatly beneficial in certain situations on protected greens when you are trying to avoid sand traps and water hazards. It could be useful for you. So get a grip folks!

Click here to leave a 5 star review!

Chapter 2: Mastering the Sequence of the Swing

There are those who believe that mastering a good golf game depends on your ability to perfectly time wrist and arm motions in your swing. While this is important, you need to know a little bit more than that. In order to have the most reliability in your swing you need to be able to master the exact sequence that will allow you to make the most of rhythm, tempo, and timing.

This is the only way you can break out of the hit or miss drudgery of someone who doesn't have their swing path down. Master the techniques presented here and you will be well on your way to forging a consistent golf swing. Breaking down the proper sequence of events in order here, is the sequence of the swing.

Use Your Swing Trigger

Just about every Pro Golfer I have ever seen always starts off their swing with some form of a swing trigger. What is a swing trigger you might ask? Have you ever seen Jack Nicklaus cock his chin to the right immediately before making a swing? Have you ever watched Tiger Woods move ever so slightly off the ball right before starting his swing?

Have you ever noticed how he moves exactly the same way every single time he leads up to hitting the golf ball? Did you think that was just some sort of repetitive, superstitious ritual? Like when a baseball player who has to spit three times and adjust himself immediately before pitching a baseball? Wrong!

These seemingly meaningless gesticulations are what each of these golfers developed in order to get themselves locked in a natural motion of consistently hitting the golf ball, relatively the same each time. Once their bodies move in this signature trigger motion it helps send their nervous system on automatic, allowing for a smooth initiation of their swing and preventing any anxious or jittery movement that would unhinge the motion.

In order to be successful, you need to find your own swing trigger that gets you in the groove. Experiment until you find what works for you and you will be a lot better off when you do!

Go to Your Takeaway

The next phase of the swing is the "takeaway". The takeaway constitutes one fluid action in which you determine the entire speed and structure of your swing. At this point in the sequence you should be moving your chest, arms, hands, and club in tandem as your club head is positioned down to the ground while your back swing looms large. In addition, this move will initiate your head away from your ball.

Orient Club head to the Right Plane

This part of the sequence should occur just a few feet into the swing, with your club moving in gradual tandem with your bal-to-target line. This orientation needs to stay well outside of your hands. To initiate this kind of swing you need to start out with your club's butt (yes, your club has a butt) so that you can then move the club toward your upper right leg helping to keep your swing in the right direction.

Open your Club Head

As you continue the motion of turning your body in your swing begin to open up the range of your club head, this means that you should be lowly turning your club head toward the right plane. Consider the head of your club to be like a door, and as you turn your body and go through the motion of the swing, you are slowly opening that door, turning it to face the golf ball you are about to strike.

Keep Your Club in Check in the Middle of Your Backswing

At this point in the sequence you need to make sure that you keep your club in check while you are in the middle of your backswing by keeping your left arm close to your torso while your right elbow is directed outside of your body, and angled toward your feet. Another thing to look out for is the posturing of your wrists. You need to make sure that your wrists are triangulating a proper formation between your club and hands.

Look to Your Right

At this point in your swing a certain amount of tension should be building inside your right leg in anticipation of hitting the golf ball. In tandem with this you should be aware of your left shoulder moving inward toward your neck. As you fall into this motion let your head turn to the right so that your spine begins to spin around. This leads up to the centrifugal motion of throwing your entire weight into your swing. This puts you in the perfect position to line up the golf ball for your shot.

Turn Your Lower Body

Your lower body should now be in full swing right along with your club. Your body is unwinding now like a coiled spring, as your arms, hand, and club are angling toward the moment of impact with the ball. At this point every fiber of your being should be ready and primed for the all important moment you strike that golf ball.

Release and Straighten Your Right Arm

As you go into your downswing, keep up the triangulation of your wrists. Now slowly open up your posture so that your line of sight increases with the downward motion and pulls your club head in sync with the golf ball. This movement will automatically flow together as you release and straighten your right arm.

Tense the Muscles on Your Left Side

At this point in the sequence you need to make sure that you are able to have just the right amount of tension in your body as it uncoils to strike the golf ball. In doing this your left side should be tensing up even while your right side is rocketing right toward impact with the golf ball. Keep your arm outstretched, with your body weight thrust moving quickly ahead, so that you can build up toward hitting the golf ball.

Make Full Rotation of Your Body as Your Club Impacts the Golf Ball

Nearing the end of the sequence your body will take advantage of its full rotation so that most of your weight will shift to the left half of your body, with your right heel digging firmly into the ground. Your knees should also slightly brush against each other as you really dig into the swing. This will help increase the ultimate acceleration as you drive your club into the golf ball.

End With Hand Raised Above Shoulder

At this point, immediately after impact, you should straighten up your body, as you return to a place of balance with your swinging arm wrapping around above your shoulder. It may not seem important what happens after the ball has already been hit (proper form won't change the direction of the ball after it has been struck!) but it is a necessary measure to keep you in good shape for your next swing.

Because believe it or not, how you end your swing can effect how you begin your *next swing*. There have actually been some golfers who have pulled muscles and seriously injured themselves by not properly ending a backswing, so it really is important to master the entire sequence from beginning to end. So even as insignificant as it may sound, even after the golf ball has already took flight over the greenway, make sure that you finish the motions that you have started by ending with your hand raised above your shoulder.

Click here to leave a review!

Chapter 3: Working On Your Posture

Remember that cranky old Middle School Health and Fitness teacher who told you not to slouch? Well it turns out they might have had a point because having proper posture could mean everything when it comes to golf. Quite simply, if your shoulders are slumped, your backswing will be slumped as well! And yet it is often among the most neglected part of most swings. Here are a few examples why working on your posture is so important.

The Pre-Address Position

When we speak in golf about the "Pre-Address" position, we are speaking of the posture you take right before you get ready to take a shot at the golf ball. This position should have you in an athletic posture with your knees gently bent and your spine as upright as possible with your shoulders rolled back. The shoulders as mentioned earlier are actually a very important part of it.

If your shoulders are slumped forward too much it will make your whole face droop down to see the ball and will not allow you to keep a steady gaze during your swing, temporarily obscuring your line of sight. Not a good thing. So keep your shoulders back so you can keep your visual line of sight with the ball intact. This will also help to stabilize your overall position making sure that your body stays in line for the duration of your swing.

Address Position

This is the position you are in right when your golf club makes contact with the ball. It is imperative that you keep good posture during this part of the process. In this position you will reach out with your left arm in order to keep this position as straight as possible, with the bottom of your club directed opposite of your armpit. At this point your knees should be bent, your weight should be on the balls of your feet, and your rear should be stuck out with your spine straightened and your shoulders pulled back. This posture will enable you to have better consistency, with stronger backswings.

Have Enough Axis Tilt at Address

In order to successfully execute from your position of good posture you need to have enough axis tilt at address. What does that mean? Basically, it just means that you need to make sure that your upper body maintains a slight lean in opposition while your leading shoulder stays just a little bit higher than the back. This is how you should achieve axis tilt.

If you can't get quite enough axis tilt, you are in danger of executing a pivot reversal, leading to many potentially bad swings. Even more disastrous than this, not having the right tilt could also throw your back out! Neglecting this aspect of posture has caused many golfers to get seriously injured, so always be sure to pay attention to how much axis tilt you employ at address. So just keep working on your posture and your golf game will work for you!

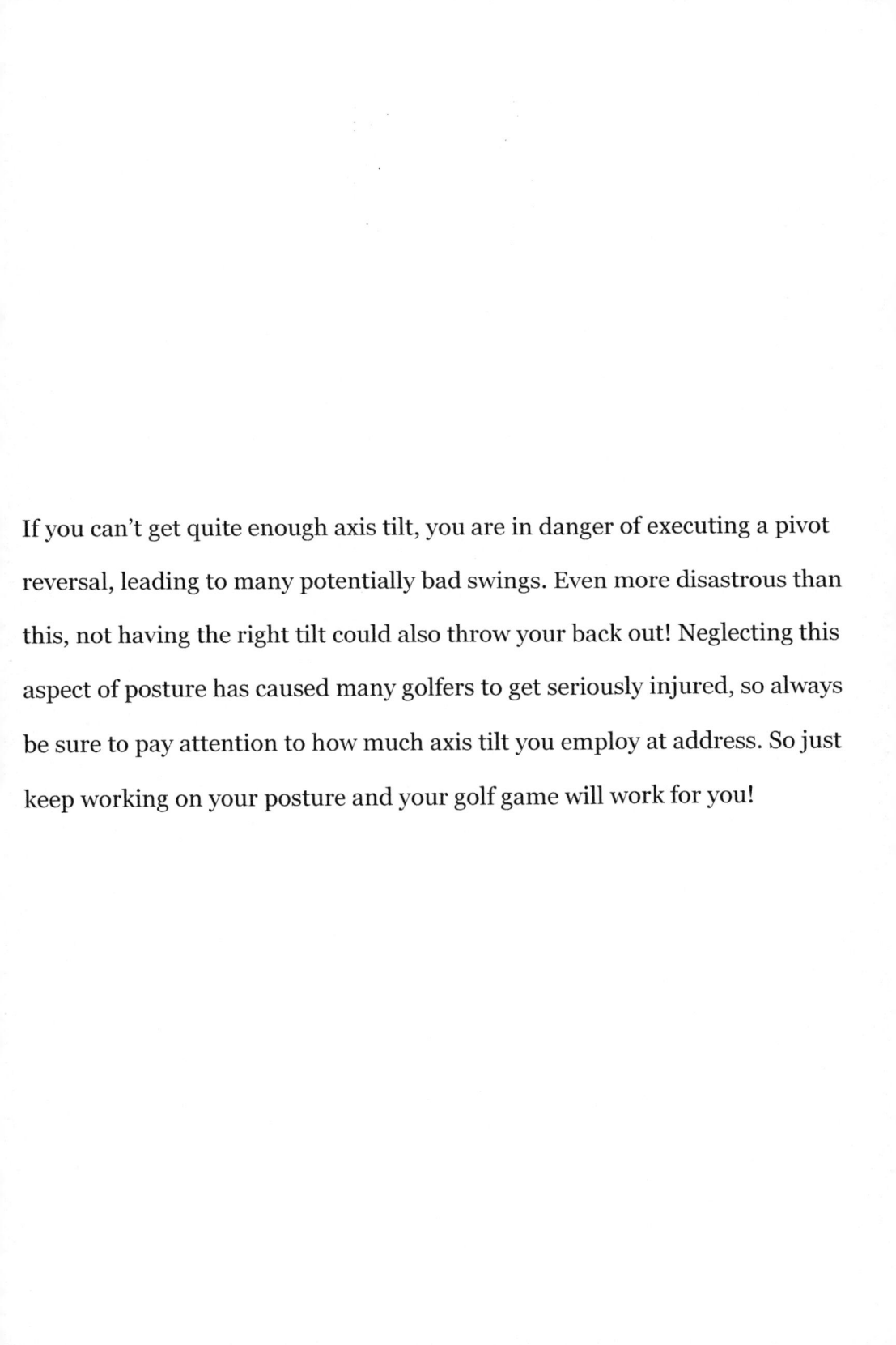

Chapter 4: The Impact of Your Type of Golf Club on Your Swing

As anyone who has played golf, or even anyone who as observed others play golf can ascertain, a golfer typically has more than one type of golf club. Golfers carry around this variety of equipment for a reason. And the type of cub you use can have a direct impact on your swing. Here are a few types of the clubs that you will deal with and how they can be of use.

Woods

Perhaps the most common type of club, "woods" based golf clubs consist of the main driver and fairway clubs. The golf clubs with the largest heads are the ones that are called "woods". These larger heads are hollow and extend a few inches across and a few inches back. Woods also usually have longer shafts and it is this fact that enables players to swing the clubs faster, producing longer shots in the process. These woods can greatly impact the overall potential and scope of your swing.

Irons

Irons are classified by number and if you have ever been out to the greenway you are probably familiar with golfers yelling to their caddies, "Hey! Get me the 9 iron!" These blubs actually range from 3 to 9 irons. But all of them have smaller club heads than their wooden counterparts do. These smaller club heads will serve a wide array of purpose for your game.

In fact when you look at them straight on, they almost look like blades, and they are sometimes referred to as such. It is the increase in number that connotes increase in loft and decreases in length. This particular variety of iron club is used for shots on the fairway or sometimes to just help facilitate tee shots for shorter duration holes.

Hybrids

These clubs are the new kids on the block and believe it or not, they have only been around since the year 2000. With the new millennium, many things changed, and were upgraded, so it was that golfers decided they needed some upgraded clubs to haul around with them in their golf carts. Much as the name implies, these clubs are a hybrid, or "cross" between both woods and irons.

These clubs are also numbered just like irons are, counting off as 1-hybrid, 2 hybrid, you get the idea. These clubs take the best of both worlds and are generally viewed to be easier to use than the more unwieldy irons and cumbersome woods. They were originally intended for beginners on s learning curve, but they have proven to be so advantageous that even the pros use them. These clubs will have a definite impact on your golf swing.

Wedges

Make a mental note folks, that's "wedges" *not wedgies*. Leave the wedgies in 9th grade gym class, we are talking about superb golf equipment here! The wedge is a versatile club for its purpose and can be broken down into a few varieties. There is the pitching wedge, the gap wedge, and the lob wedge. The wedge gulf club has an iron head, just like a standard iron but it is shaped different with a sharper angle or "wedge" that gives them a much shorter approach vector when it comes to operating on the greenway and navigating through sand traps.

It is the aptly named "sand wedge" that serves to aid the golfer out of the aforementioned sand traps. While the pitching wedge is the one that is used to send the golf ball out on far afield, and is the most common of all wedges to be found. The gap wedge is a combination of the pitching wedge and the sand wedge falling somewhere in the "gap" between the two of them, having more loft than a pitching wedge, yet not as much as a sand wedge.

The lob wedge on the other hand has the highest loft of all and is good for steep angles. This works well for trick shots over hilly terrain or when having to navigate through surprise obstacles like treetops! I have personally used a lob wedge myself with much the same result, so I can vouch for the voracity of it. This will definitely impact your swing!

Sign up to stay up-to-date with Paul Meyer's latest books!

Chapter 5: Understanding the Concept of a Swing Plane

Whenever a golfer hears a reference to the "swing plane" you can be sure that confusion isn't far behind. But finally, here in the chapter of this book we are going to take on this often confused concept and break it down for you in an easy to understand manner. Here are the basics of what you need to know when it comes to the utilization of the swing plane.

Two Planes of Golfing Existence!

Basically, the idea of the swing plane is used to categorize and distinguish the spatial planes from which the club is swung. For example, someone who is a "one-plane" swinger then they are swinging their club in line with their shoulders and keeping all of their movement in that "one" single plane of space where they are making their swing.

But if someone is a "two-planer" the swing is much, much more of a steep incline than it otherwise would be and the shoulder is dropped in order to strike the golf ball. While the golfer who resides on "one-plane" launches forward at the ball like a tennis-player, it is the "two-plane" golfer who uses more of a lifting motion, almost like they are digging right into the ground.

Mastering the One-Plane Method

If you are going to work out of the one-plane then you need to figure out how you can keep yourself inside of a one-plane box without falling way too flat. You will mot likely need to apply considerably more force in your downswing in order to achieve this. This allows the club to fall behind you, and reveals the face of the club considerably.

Another way to achieve this is to drop your downswing rather hard and drop your right arm all the way down while keeping your forearm in rotation, pointed at your feet. This will keep your within the surface area of the one-plane during your golf swing. By staying within these boundaries you are creating a habitual safe zone for you to fall back on as your default.

Mastering the Two-Plane Method

By residing inside two planes the golfer has really use their hips as they swing in order to produce enough brute force to remain consistent. These players tend to raise their golf clubs up high at the beginning of the swing, but refrain from turning their hips. But this is a grave mistake, and will only serve to restrict their range movement.

In order to generate enough strength and reach they need to move their hips in sync with their swing. In order to be successful with the two-plane method you need to keep your left forearm in right front of you. Allow the weight of your golf club to generate the massive up and down movement you require.

Which Swing Plane is Best?

It really depends on the player and the situations that they face. The best way to ascertain what might be best is to take a few factors into consideration. Are you flexible? If the answer is yes, and you also happen to have pretty good upper body that's prone to swinging the club with more aggression, then you should probably stick to one-plane.

But if don't happen to be very flexible and you don't tend to put as much power and enthusiasm behind your swings then you should consider working within a two-plane mode of operation. Every player has their own sweet spot when it comes to the swing-plane, but it is the really good players that learn how to successfully navigate between the two.

So to answer the question which swing plane is best? Both of them are best! You just have to know how and when to use them to their fullest potential.

The best golf players are able to effortlessly switch between the too. You will no doubt find such a feat difficult just starting out, but if you keep at it, you will learn how to do the same.

Chapter 6: Keeping Up the Proper Pace, Rhythm, and Tempo

Did you know that you are keeping count to a tempo every single time you swing a golf club? You may not realize it, but you are setting your pace even as you cut your club through the air. Its just that not everyone's temp is as in-sync as others. But even if your internal clock is a little bit off, there is always time to fine tune it. This will enable you to reduce your low scoring handicaps and move the ball much further afield than you would have been able to do otherwise.

Although tempo is often the unsung hero of golf it is still absolutely crucial to maintaining a good swing. You can adjust your tempo at will by swinging slow, fast, or neutral. Tempo is usually hard to teach because it is something so intuitive that the golfer has to just feel it out, and see what comes naturally to them. Much of golf is a completely hands on learning process

If you are a complete beginner, this means that you just need to experiment and practice with your pace until it seems that you have come across the exact tempo that works for you. But if you are really having trouble trying to figure out in what tempo you are living in, you can try a little experiment to help steer yourself in the right direction.

The Tempo Test

First, take about four balls and line them all up in a row. Now stand in front of the one that is nearest, and then proceed to hit it with about ¼ of your normal strength. Now move on down the line to the next ball and proceed to hit it at 50 percent capacity. You are now at half speed, so let's just keep it moving along and see what kind of tempo we end up with.

Next, as you may have guessed, hit the third ball at about 75% strength and then of course, ball number four at 100% full strength. Pay close attention to how you felt at each of these varying speeds and then make note of the ball that seemed to work out well for you. This test will help you ascertain your natural built-in tempo.

Build Rhythm

Rhythm is the natural fluidity of your swing in motion, helping you to create more consistency in your swing. The most challenging part of doing this is maintaining proper pace between the downswing and the backswing. This should be one sweeping motion between the two, but there is often choppiness, and a pause that throws off the rhythm. To avoid this, think about what you are doing, and try to count time in your head.

It may sound strange but try using phrases such as "back and through", "slow and low" just to keep yourself in time. If it helps, you might also want to practice swinging your club in the darkness so that you can learn to feel the swing and its timing, more than simply watching with your eyes. As you shadow learn like this you can then remember the motions that you rehearsed when you are out on the golf course and intuitively know how to build up your own unique rhythm.

Click here to leave a review!

Sign up to stay up-to-date with Paul Meyer's latest books!

Chapter 7: Making the Best of Your Stance, Alignment and Footwork.

In this chapter let's go over some basic strategies to improve our stance, alignment, and our footwork. These are all simple concepts but they are crucial to your success. We will go over each of them in depth and with no consideration whatsoever to your previous skill level or expertise. No matter how long you've been playing golf try to look at the examples presented here with a pair of fresh, new eyes.

Stance

If you ever doubt that whether or not you are maintaining a proper stance while you golf, all you need to do to check your status is to position yourself in imitation of a direct shot. Because if you position yourself as if you are about to inflict a direct hit on the golf ball, you will have to automatically have to move to the left (to the right if you are left handed, sorry lefties!) in order to maintain your line of sight. You left side will know be in slight variance with the golf ball, this variance is a key indicator of your own flexibility and equilibrium in the stance that you have taken on.

Alignment

Your alignment, much as the name might imply, helps you to stay *in line* with the ball. The exact alignment that you take on will vary a bit according to your body type. So, based on your height, weight, and general shape, the alignment you choose will differ from the alignment of someone else. Everyone else you encounter on the golf course will have a slightly different disposition.

It's just like a car has different alignments in order to represent the diversity in car frames, so does the human constitution. This means that you need to find an alignment that works for you. But although some experimentation is required, as a cardinal rule, in order to keep your line of sight correct, you will always need to usually stay a little bit left of center.

Footwork

And last but certainly not least in this book, I wanted to reserve some space to deal with proper footwork. The feet are probably the most neglected part of the human body when it comes to mastering a good swing in golf. People usually focus on the twists and turns of the torso, and the movement of the arms, and shoulders; forgetting all about feet!

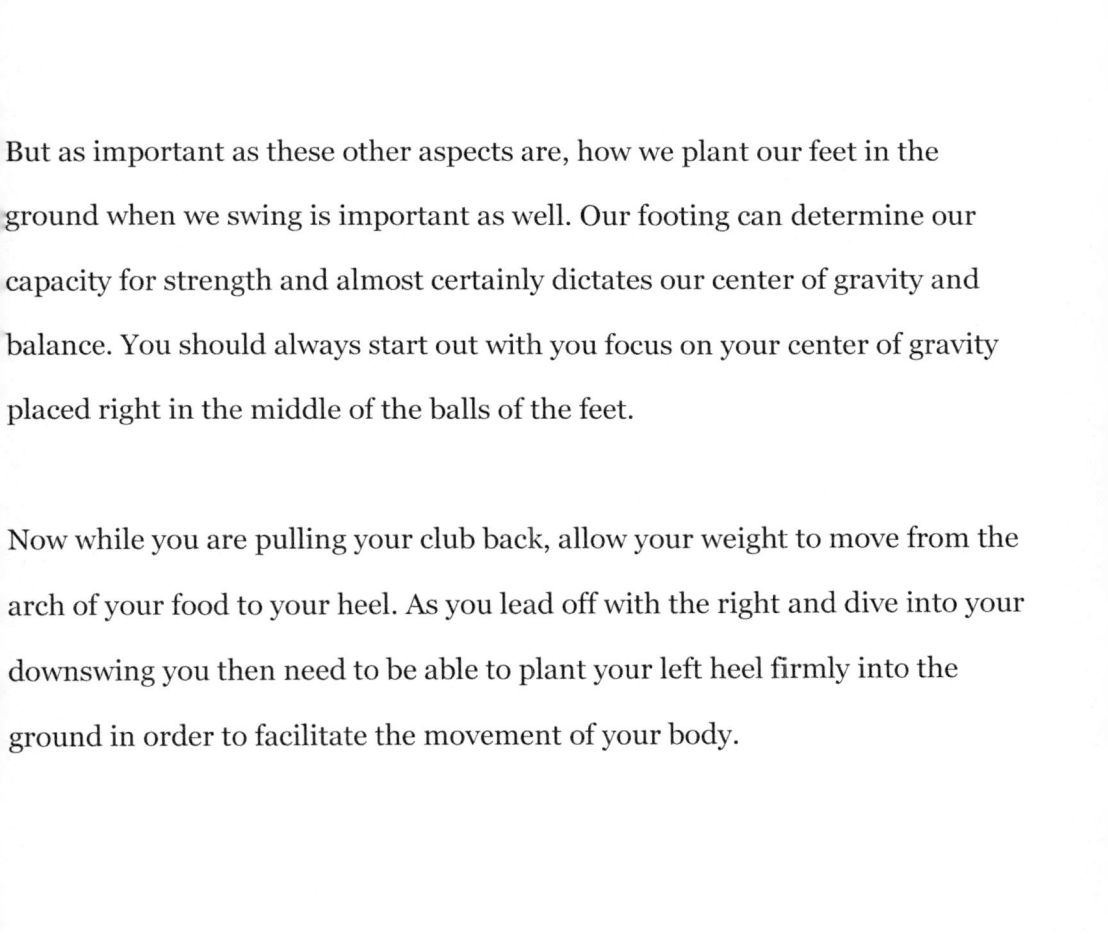

But as important as these other aspects are, how we plant our feet in the ground when we swing is important as well. Our footing can determine our capacity for strength and almost certainly dictates our center of gravity and balance. You should always start out with you focus on your center of gravity placed right in the middle of the balls of the feet.

Now while you are pulling your club back, allow your weight to move from the arch of your food to your heel. As you lead off with the right and dive into your downswing you then need to be able to plant your left heel firmly into the ground in order to facilitate the movement of your body.

Conclusion: It's Elementary my Dear Watson

Bubba Watson has recently taken the world of golf by storm. Not since Tiger Woods has someone captivated the golf course with his downswing. You would think that Bubba was simply born with these incredible moves. But in reality, just like everyone else this champion golfer had to take the time to learn and refine his trade. If you were to watch someone like Bubba Watson in slow motion you would see all of the strange little idiosyncrasies that make up the whole package that is Bubba Watson's golf swing.

The man seems at first to squat down really low but then jumps backward as soon as he makes impact. Bubba's moves may seem a bit unorthodox but they work for him. Bubba knows the fundamentals of golf that make his eccentricities work. Sometimes we just make things far more complicated than they are.

It is for this reason that I sincerely hope that this book has served to simplify some of the most basic tenants of golf. Once you get down those basic fundamental steps and start experimenting from the ground up, take it from

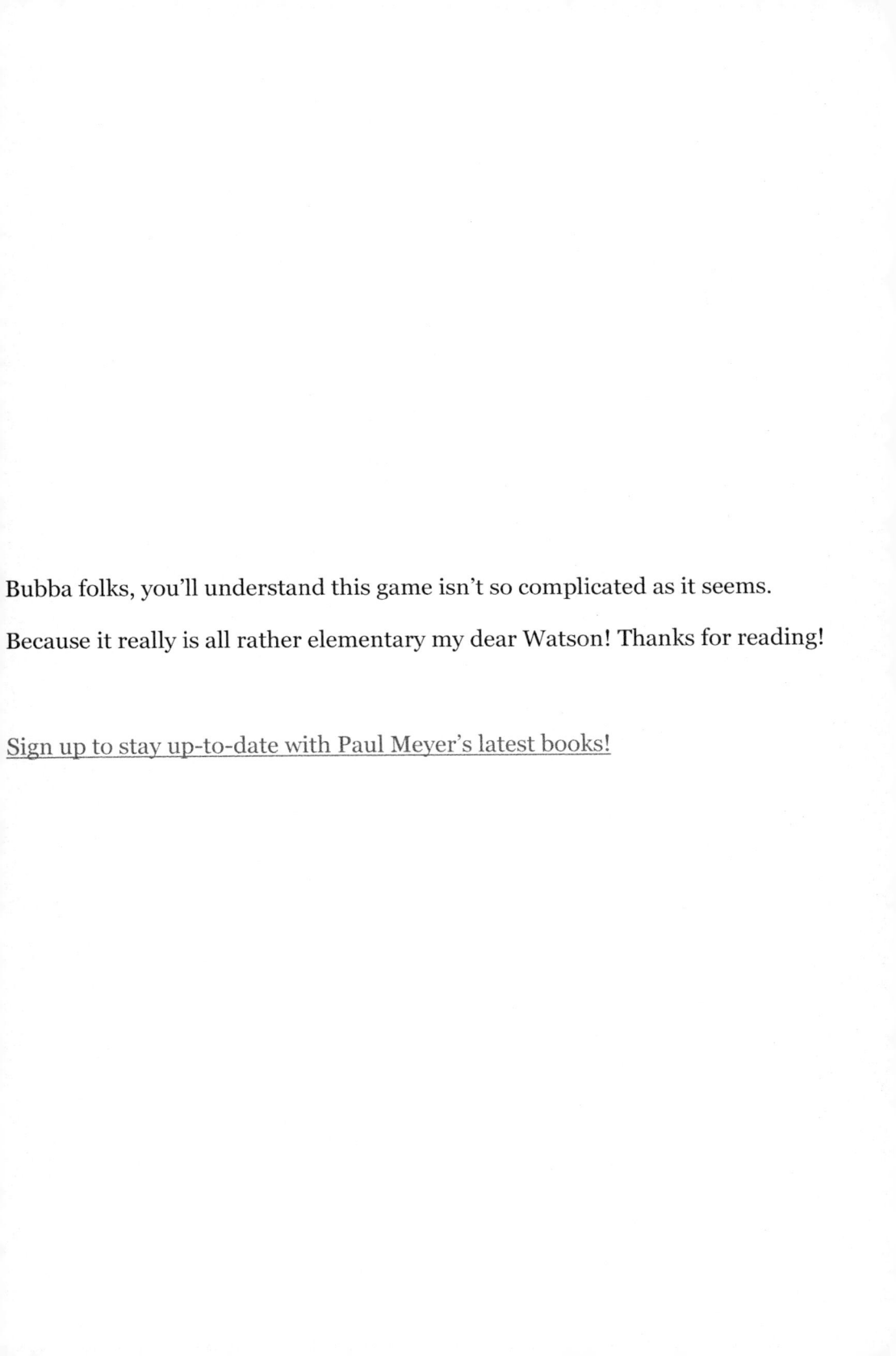

Bubba folks, you'll understand this game isn't so complicated as it seems.

Because it really is all rather elementary my dear Watson! Thanks for reading!

Sign up to stay up-to-date with Paul Meyer's latest books!

Printed in Great Britain
by Amazon